Table of Contents

Meet Ivan Chermayeff

Ivan Chermayeff at work

Ivan Chermayeff makes books about fish. He also helps make aquariums! You can find Mr. Chermayeff's art in aquariums all over the world.

Inside an aquarium Mr. Chermayeff helped build

A fish mural by Mr. Chermayeff

For
Loulou
Fanny
& Phinney

Ivan Chermayeff

Fishy Facts

Conceived and Written by
Catherine Chermayeff and Nan Richardson

Acknowledgments

For each of the selections listed below, grateful acknowledgment is made for permission to excerpt and/or reprint original or copyrighted material, as follows:

Text

1 *Fishy Facts*, by Ivan Chermayeff, Catherine Chermayeff and Nan Richardson. Text copyright © 1994 by Ivan Chermayeff, Catherine Chermayeff and Nan Richardson. Illustrations copyright © 1994 by Ivan Chermayeff. Reprinted by permission of Harcourt Brace & Company. **36** "There Was a Fish," from *The Sweet and Sour Animal Book*, by Langston Hughes. Copyright © 1994 by Ramona Bass and Arnold Rampersad. Reprinted by permission of Oxford University Press. **38** "Leaping Flying Fish," by Koson, from *Red Dragonfly on My Shoulder*, by Sylvia Cassedy. Copyright © 1992 by the estate of Sylvia Cassedy and Kunihiro Suetake. Reprinted by permission of HarperCollins Publishers.

Photography

i Ralph A. Clevenger/Westlight. **ii** Richard Howard (tl); Y. Matsumura/Cambridge Seven Associates (bl, r); Banta Digital Group (background). **32** © Mike Severns/Tony Stone Images (l); John Gorman/FPG (m). **32/33** Keith Philpott/Image Bank (background). **33** © Steven Frink/Tony Stone Images. **34** Steven Frink/Stock Market (t); Steven Frink/Tony Stone Images (b). **34-35** Romilly Lockyer/The Image Bank (background). **35** Steinhart Aquarium/Photo Researchers (tl); © Steven Frink/Tony Stone Images (r). **38** Bridgeman/Art Resource, NY.

1997 Impression

Houghton Mifflin Edition, 1996
Copyright © 1996 by Houghton Mifflin Company. All rights reserved.

Printed in the U.S.A.

ISBN 0-395-73164-X

789-B-98 97 96

HOUGHTON MIFFLIN COMPANY
BOSTON
ATLANTA   DALLAS   GENEVA, ILLINOIS   PALO ALTO   PRINCETON

Zebrafish can change color to match their surroundings.

3

The sawfish cuts up other fish into bite-size pieces
with the sharp, toothed edges of its snout.

The parrotfish's
teeth grow together
to make a beak
like a bird's,
which it uses to
bite into coral.

7

When the male toadfish grunts,

he is as loud as a subway train.

9

The flounder is a nearly flat fish that lies
on the sandy bottom of inlets and bays.
Both of its eyes look up
from the same side of its head.

11

Muscles in its long tail make electricity, which it uses to stun prey.

The goosefish has a mouth
that is nearly as wide as its body.
A lure hangs from a spine
in front of its teeth to
attract small fish.

15

As they put their mouths together
and appear to kiss, grunts grind their teeth
and make piglike noises.

The hammerhead shark
swims quickly
as it chases its prey.

Its eyes are far
apart on the sides
of its head.

The butterfly fish has an "eyespot" near its tail that makes it hard for other fish to tell its head from its tail.

21

The lantern fish lives in the depths of the sea during the day, but rises to the surface at night.

The spots along its body
glow in the dark.

With tiny side fins and a little tail,
the cowfish is a very slow swimmer.

When the puffer
is afraid, it swallows
lots of water or air
and blows itself up
into a prickly ball
too large for most
other fish to swallow.

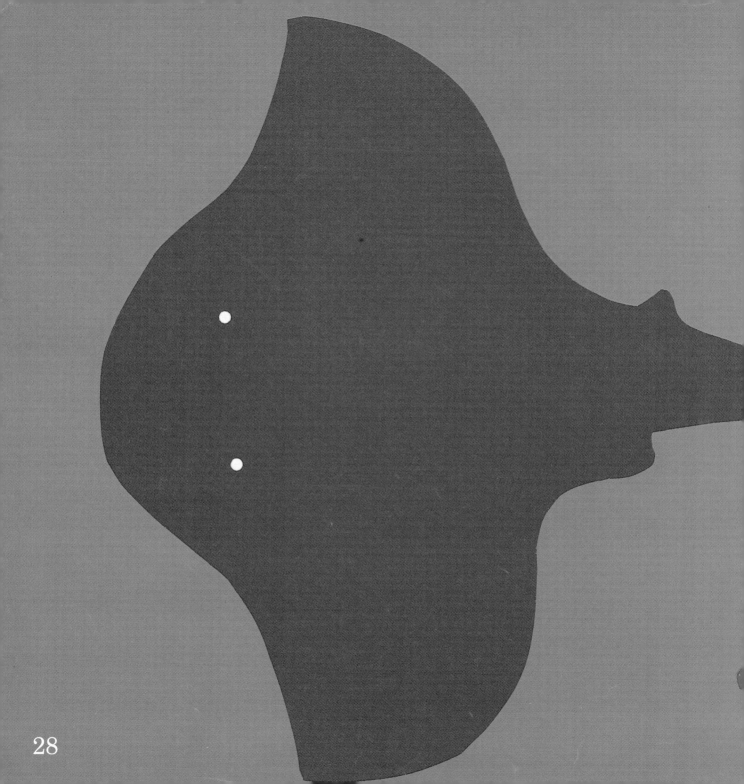

The stingray has a stinger on its long, thin tail.
It rests on the bottom of the ocean,
hidden in the sand, and only stings if it
is disturbed or frightened.

After

a mother sea horse

lays her eggs,

the father sea horse

carries them

in his pouch

until they hatch

and the babies

swim out.

Fishy

How are these photos different
from the drawings in *Fishy Facts*?
How are they the same?

parrotfish

cowfish

Photos

puffer

butterfly fish

toadfish

goosefish

sea horse

There Was a Fish

by Langston Hughes

f

There was a fish
With a greedy eye
Who darted toward
A big green fly.

36

Fish art by students from the Harlem School of the Arts

Alas! That fly
Was bait on a hook!
So the fisherman took
The fish home to cook.

The Golden Fish by Paul Klee

Leaping flying fish!
Dancing for me and my boat
as I sail for home.

A haiku by Kôson